TRANSFORMING

in

GOD'S PLAN

A Collection of Poems

by

MEI ESTHER WANG

Mei Esther Wang • Alhambra, CA

TRANSFORMING IN GOD'S PLAN
PUBLISHED BY MEI ESTHER WANG

ISBN-13:
978-0692206744
ISBN-10:
0692206744

Cover design by Anthony Duhamel Jr.
Cover photos by Stephen Russell Smith, Shutterstock

Printed in the United States of America
First Edition

I dedicate this book to my Lord and my friends Anthony and Rachel that helped to make my dream come true. I appreciate Sam who was with me when I was attacked and in the hospital. I appreciate Wajid Ali who was with me after Sam was gone until now. All of you have shown me true friendship when I was down and gave me a helping hand so that I could get back on my feet again. May God remember you and bless you abundantly.

CONTENTS

FOREWORD

It's amazing what God can do when His children come together to accomplish something in His name. The Bible says, "For where two or three gather in my name, there am I with them" *(Matthew 18:20 NIV)*. God's presence was very apparent in my first meeting with Ms. Wang and continues to be every time my wife and I have met with her in order to get this book out into the world. Lifting up the name of Jesus has been and will always be the number one goal of this project and our future collaborations with Mei that are sure to come.

It's not everyday that you meet somebody that completely transforms your thinking, strengthens your faith, and inspires you to become a better person overall. Mei Esther Wang has been that person for me and my wife since the first day that we met her and every hour that we have spent with her since. I know that Mei greatly appreciates our help in getting this book designed and published, but I don't think she will ever fully know the profound impact that her spirit and her love of Jesus has had and will forever have on our lives and the lives of the people that are blessed with the opportunity to read her poetry.

Everything that Mei does and everything that she has been through points to Jesus. In a world and a time where it is so easy to get caught up in our own struggles and our own race to the finish line, it takes a chance meeting with someone like Mei to put everything in perspective. In my own walk with the Lord, there have been ups and downs and blessings and trials, and my faith and strength wavers more than I would like to admit. As much as we read and receive the promises of God, the things we see in the natural realm often blind us to spiritual truths. Mei is the embodiment of the verse, "For we walk by faith, and not by sight" *(2 Corinthians 5:7 KJV)*. No matter what obstacles she is overcoming or what giants have attempted to block her path in life, she has learned to cling to the promises of God and stand on His Word.

As a follower of Christ, Mei's faith has time and time again served to strengthen my own. Editing this book together has been one of the greater experiences of my life and walk with Jesus. To see and understand what she has been through and the fruit that has grown out of her toughest times has been a blessing beyond measure.

As a person, her determination and passion for life and education puts my greatest efforts and accomplishments to shame. Her tenacity motivates me to accomplish more of my own goals and dreams, regardless of the roadblocks that life throws my way. "God sends rain on the just and the unjust alike" *(Matthew 5:45 NLT)*, and we would all be much better off to take a page from Mei's life and use it as instructions of how to live out our own. It is my hope that you are as blessed by your encounter with Ms. Wang as we were with ours.

- Anthony Duhamel Jr.

PREFACE

"Just when the caterpillar thought his life was over...he became a butterfly and began to fly." - Author unknown

I always dreamed of becoming a writer, which is why my bachelor's degree is in English literature. However, my life went through some dramatic changes. I have always had to struggle to survive and have not had the time to make my dreams come true until now. My parents passed away when I was fifteen years old. Although this age should be old enough to take care of yourself, it was very difficult for a young woman in a wheelchair.

I have had polio since the age of one, and it causes my spine to be deformed. When I was a child, I had many surgeries, and my mother would always stay by my side during my recovery. I had a major surgery on my spine, shortly after my parents passed away, and now I was all alone, lying on a cold bed with a large wound spanning from the top of my neck to the base of my spine. It took me two years to recover from this surgery.

After my recovery, I went to work at a factory as an assembly line operator, but I have always loved to learn and never gave up on going back to finish high school and obtain a college degree. After a few years of working at the factory, I met a couple that connected me with a Christian missionary organization that gave me the opportunity to finish my schooling. I was able to live at a special facility for people with disabilities and go to school everyday for three years to finally get my high school diploma.

From there, I was able to attend Christ College in Taiwan to get my first college degree. I still remember the difficulty of getting myself to and from class everyday. The school was in the mountains, and the road from my dormitory to the campus was treacherous. Back then, I was able to use crutches, so you can imagine the hike I had to endure everyday. However, after four years of hard work and overcoming many obstacles, I graduated with a Bachelor's degree. That was a proud day for me.

The most challenging part of my life was migrating to the United States to continue my studies and obtain a Master's Degree. Although I knew that moving across the world to a new country completely on my own would be a challenge, my passion for learning has always motivated me to move forward. The language barrier, my disability, financial difficulties, immigration and green card issues, and the lack of family support in this new country made my previous obstacles in life seem very small. After many years of traveling, hard work, and lack of sleep, I obtained a Master's Degree in Special Education from Azusa Pacific University and a second Master's Degree in Rehabilitation Counseling from California State University Los Angeles. At that time in my life, I was very proud of the new chapter I had started and was excited about the bright future that I had ahead of me. Little did I know that the most difficult stage was yet to come.

The first job that I got after finishing my Master's Degree did not turn out the way that I had hoped, and my employer refused to sponsor me for a green card to stay in the United States. For many immigrants, this is a very difficult hurdle in obtaining citizenship. Many people don't realize how difficult it is to find a job that comes with legal sponsorship or an employer that will sponsor you once you are hired. After losing my legal working status in the United States, I had no choice but to continue my search for sponsored employment and live off of the little savings that I had left. Inevitably, I ran out of money and opportunities and could not afford my rent any longer. In 2009, I became homeless.

Although I am disabled, I am a dedicated and educated woman. I am not ashamed about this time in my life, and I am proud of myself for how I dealt with the situation. By the grace of God, I was able to find a homeless shelter that had accommodations for my disability. Unfortunately, each shelter has a policy which only allows you to stay for a limited time, so I had to be transferred to different shelters many times over a three-year period. As a disabled woman in a wheelchair, traveling and carrying my belongings from place to place was very difficult.

"And we know that all things work together for good to those who love God and have been called according to His purpose" *(Romans 8:28 NIV)*. Never was that more real to me than in my third year of homelessness. My blessing in disguise came in 2012 when I was attacked by a man on the train. I still don't know why the man attacked me, but I know that God took something that was meant to destroy me and used it for good. The attack was bad and my injuries put me in the hospital. The police were involved in the incident, which helped bring to light some of the other discriminations that I had been dealing with over the last few years. As a result of the attack, I was able to get an attorney to appeal for me to receive a special Victim Visa in order to allow me to legally stay in the United States. Praise the Lord, my Victim Visa was approved just before Christmas last year (2013). It was the best Christmas gift I ever received!

In addition to receiving my Victim Visa, I was also transferred to a more permanent public nursing home as a result of the attack, and I am still living there today. Although I am still continuing my education and my search for employment so that I can provide for myself and live in my own home, I am so thankful that the Lord has provided for me this way.

People often ask me, "Why did you stay in the U.S. to suffer on the streets, with no job, no home, and no legal status for so long? Why didn't you go back to your home country and live a better life?" I am sure you are asking this same question as you read my story, so here is my answer.

Before I decided to come to the U.S., I had already been praying for this for a long time, and it was clear to me that it was God's will for me to come here. Although I have been through many extremes and hardships, I still believe and keep my faith in God. I never wanted to use a quickie marriage or any of my own ways to get a Green Card. God revealed to me a long time ago that as long as I did my best in my schooling and my work, He would take care of my needs. Sometimes, it is so hard to keep my faith. When the night is dark for so long and waiting seems hopeless, I have to push myself to choose to believe in God again.

Whether the hardships come from the devil or from ignorant people along my path, I know that if I can stay strong that eventually God is going to show them that He is almighty and nobody can defeat Him and His children. Since I have this faith and this vision for my life, I can cooperate with God and endure in the waiting. In the meantime, God uses my hardships to transform my heart and my character. I wrote this collection of poems at different points over the last few years of my journey, and it is my hope that they illustrate my journey with God and strengthen your own faith as you read them. Praise be to God for His wisdom, His grace, and His eternal love for us forever and ever!

- Mei Esther Wang *3/24/2014*

I Know That I Am Loved By God

I have done my best
I have lived my life

I am unique and special
The most beloved by God

I have run my race,
I have an eternal reward waiting for me

No more tears and sorrow
In heaven God embraces me

     In His loving arms

8/12/2011

LORD! PLEASE LISTEN TO MY PRAYER

Oh, Lord I pray to you
With all my heart
Make me humble so I can see
Your endless love

Send me as your messenger
To show people who you are
Open my eyes and others' so that we can see
The eternal but not the now

All the human history just repeating
And finally ending somehow
Wasting our energy on playing games
Only for temporary lust

Forgetting that we are created by God
For divine purpose and love
Only pure and true love can resolve our chaos
And guide our way home

Forever joy, peace, and transformation
More than we can ever know

8/15/2011

I Am A Dreamer Day And Night

I am a dreamer day and night
Hoping for the world to be a better place
No sorrow, tears, pain or goodbyes
There is no such place on earth

Wondering why humans need to suffer
The Spirit tells me that everything is temporary
I'm making a difference starting with me
I am still a dreamer day and night

Hoping heaven comes down
And the old world will be replaced with the new

9/2/2011

SEARCH AND FOLLOW JESUS

Before dawn
Is the darkest

Searching for the sun
We never give up

The light will come
To break the darkness

Following the Son
We never give up

9/4/2011

How Important To Have True Friends In Our Life

A true friend will give you advice
When you are in trouble
A true friend will be happy with you
When you succeed

A true friend will lift you up
When you are down
A true friend will encourage you
When you are confused

A true friend will support you
When no one else agrees
A true friend will be there for you
When you are in pain

A true friend will cry with you
When you've lost a true love

9/5/2011

Do Not Be Discouraged

I have learned to stay away
From people who give me

Negative words, thoughts
And violent behaviors

Instead, I turned these around
To my strong will power and faith

My heart
Is the only real thing

Others are fading
Passing away like an illusion

11/6/2011

A SPECIAL LADY, MY MOTHER

She was the first one I loved
Since I left her womb and opened my eyes
She was the first one who helped
Me with my first step

She was the one who suffered
Along with me when I was in the hospital
She was exhausted and fell asleep
By my hospital bed without a cover

She was the one who carried me
On her back to school and to home
She was the one who cried louder than me
When I could not play with other kids

She was the one who smiled
With great tears in her eyes
When I would receive
A good grade from school

She was the one who sewed
My clothes when she was getting old
Even with her poor vision
And only a threading needle

She was the one who was so ill
Suffering from cancer and still
Worried about my well-being
And about my marriage

She was an angel sent from God
And now has returned to heaven
She was my mother and she was
The greatest one in the world

I miss her so much
She was a special lady
And she will always remain
Here in my heart

5/12/2012

TRUST IN GOD

I cannot sleep
Because I don't want to sleep
I am afraid that I will miss
Any chances to watch your steps

I am always standing by your side
Sharing your happiness
I am crying with you
When you are in deep sorrows

You never know
Because you never follow your heart
Now even worse than that
You have totally lost your heart

You cannot hurt me any more
Because my heart's already full of scars
I cannot repair my heart
Unless I submit it to God

Once I obey God
I know that He is in control
Just trust in God
I want to say that again

Trust in God

5/22/2012

HALF & HALF

Life is half real
And half fantasy

Entertainment is half inspiring
And half depressing

Knowledge is half wise
And half confused

Art is half spiritual
And half naked truth

People are half true
And half fake

But only touch
One person's heart

Then life is completed
As a whole

5/30/2012

MEMORY

You are my memories
My memories are all you
Wherever I go, whatever I do
I am sick but nobody can heal me

I hope I can disappear
If that's what you wish
My family and friends
Are calling me but far away

I am lost and feel so empty
I hope I can disappear
If that's what you wish
God please help me

6/3/2012

TASTE IT

Life is tough
Challenge it

Life is hurt
Learn from it

Life is good
Enjoy it

Life is temptation
Overcome it

Life is sweet
But only against the sour

You must have
A sensitive tongue

To taste it

6/4/2012

Pure Loving Hearts

A true love doesn't need
To compare to one another

A true love cannot be copied
Because a copy won't last long

A true love isn't jealous
But only wishes the best

A true love is as simple as this
Pure and compassionate

God knows our heart
He will work it out for two

Pure loving hearts

6/15/2012

TORNADO LOVE

Blessed are the hearts
That are broken
They are healed and strengthened
By God's mercy and love

They become stronger

Than ever

6/15/2012

WE ARE GOD'S MESSENGER

We are the messenger
Sent by God
To tell the world
About His love

Strengthened by
His almighty power
Brave like a soldier
Tender like a dove

Passing through
This wicked world
Looking for
Our fallen people

We have nothing
To boast except
That God is
Our only hope

It's our obligation
To bring and lead
And guide lost people
To our God

Eternal peace and joy
Are the greatest reward

6/24/2012

LIFE IS...

Life is like a stock market
If you invest wisely
You can choose a stock
With very good potential

Although the current market price
Is lower than you'd like
Know in your heart
That it will rise up soon

Life is like writing your own book
You decide how many chapters you want
It's up to you if it is a tragedy
Or a story with a happy ending

Life is like a game
When you decide to play fair
You will grow and learn
And overcome each challenge

When you decide to be greedy
You play a dangerous game
Like a gambling addict
You can never really win

6/29/2012

A City Traveler

I live in a big city
You have no idea what it looks like

Walking into the crowd
My mind flies into the clouds
Many people surround you
Yet loneliness is still all around

There is plenty of fun – you can call it that
Parties, dancing, and night clubs
You hear men and women laughing
And no one cares that you're crying

It is dark – you can call it that
Stealing, robbing, and raping on the streets
Everyone pretends nothing happened
And ignores it all

It is weird—you can call it that
I like to walk down the street at night
Look into every house's living room light
It warms my heart to imagine how happy they are

I live in a big city
You have no idea what it looks like

7/6/2012

33

CHALLENGES

We meet many challenges
Every day
You can choose to overcome them
Or you can choose to withdraw

We meet many challenges
Every day
You can choose to go back and find an easier way
Or you can choose to roll with it

You have the right
To make your own choice
Even God respects your choice
So why shouldn't I?

Just remember that
We take responsibility
Whatever the consequences
Keep your faith in God

Sometimes the choice we made
Doesn't work out right away
But in God's perfect plan
Everything will be worked out

In the end

7/23/2012

GOD KNOWS EVERYTHING

Not everyone who says
I love you
Is true
Time will prove everything

Not everyone who says
I will stay by your side forever
Is true
Circumstances will prove everything

Not everyone who says
You are my soul
Is true
Controlling egos will prove everything

Not everyone who says
I care about you
Is true
Curiosity and confusion will prove everything

But God knows Everything

    Amen!

7/24/2012

MISS YOU, MISS YOU NOT

It's not easy
To meet someone
And fall in love
With that person

It's more difficult
To forget someone
You already love
Very, very deeply

Don't listen to others
And blame yourself
When they tell you to move on
And erase it from your memory

Time is the best medicine
To heal all the wounds
Your own timing and happiness
Is the most important thing

8/14/2012

LET GO

Letting go is difficult
To all kinds of people
But all of our lives
Are so full of adventure

If the past is forever gone
Holding on only brings more pain
Let go of your sense of protection
And step out from under the umbrella

You will find a big, colorful world
Just waiting for you
Only then will you realize
How far you can fly

    Far, far away

8/18/2012

Only Me And My Love

My love is my sun shining
Upon my face to make me smile
My love is my rain falling down
Washing out my pain

My love is my river taking me
To a world of dreams
A world with only my love and me
And it's more than enough

10/14/2012

I AM, YOU ARE

I am your flower
You are my dew
Without you
I cannot bloom

I am your rainbow
You are my storm
Without you
I cannot appear

I am your angel
You are my master
Without you
I cannot function

10/15/2012

YOU ARE NOT KILLING ME, BUT YOURSELF

You know where
God and the sun is
But you choose to stay
In the darkness again

It's your choice
So never complain
About God, other people
And your difficult life again

You can never see
Through a person's soul
If you are not the one
Who is meant to be their soulmate

You can try to be a copy
But it won't last long
The only one who stays
Is the one who is meant to be

It's been proven
That you like to change your mind
Always struggling between benefits
And your true soulmate

If you choose benefits
Then don't waste your time and energy
And all of your numerous attempts
To approach me again

You threw away the true love
And treated it as a sickness
You made a joke of it
As if it's a big victory

You make a fool of yourself
But foolishly are never aware

11/3/2012

LOVE IS THE KEY

Love is the key
To all confusion and hardship
When we love ourselves
We see our value in God's eyes

Love is a guide
To the way to help others
When we love other people
We see the wisdom in God's mind

Love is a boomerang
It always comes back to us
When we help others
We are actually helping ourselves

11/12/2012

WE ARE THE CHOSEN ONE

A true believer's life is a mystery
In the whole universe
However God never tries to hide
His incredible plan from us

It's been written that our lives
Have sufferings and trials
Only through faith in Jesus
Can we receive peace

We are chosen people and must be tested
As gold is purified through fierce fire
Satan's followers and ignorant people
Like roaring lions, surround us

All who follow Jesus
Are called to be tight together
Yet many are misled by confusion
Isolation, manipulation, and temptation

It's so heavy to carry our own cross
Without any sign of hope in the darkness
Through constant prayer and strong faith
In the Lord, God shows us the way

The Lord will provide all we need
Including our prayer companions
Together we hold hands walking
Through the paths of our pilgrimage

11/26/2012

THE MEANING OF LIFE IS LOVE AND HAPPINESS

Life is a love journey
Not a pursuit of worldly success

A happy and beautiful life is always
Full of hope, surprise and thanksgiving

12/8/2012

LOVE IS A RELATIONSHIP, NOT A TEST

If we keep testing God's love
We actually don't respect Him
We don't need Him
And believe we are independent
In this case, God will respect our choice
And let us be our own master

If we keep testing
All existing relationships in our life
We actually never start or establish,
Build up or develop our relationships with others
In this case, our relationships are predictable
They won't stay very long

1/12/2013

JESUS IS THE LIGHT

In the devil's point of view
God has granted him the power
To do whatever he wants
And the dawn will never come

Since they are not the true believers
They cannot see the spiritual things
God allows bad things to happen
In order to use it for good

God keeps writing down
All things in His Book of Life
True believers trust in God
All the time to the end

And nothing can separate
The love between them and God
They also believe that
God has immeasurable wisdom

He works all things out
And as a whole
They form a beautiful picture
Only in His perfect timing

1/12/2013

FEARS CANNOT DEFEAT US

Our courage can overcome
Our fears which are not real
Only illusions in our thoughts

Our potential and will power
Are beyond our measurement

1/17/2013

TRUE LOVE HAS NO REASON

True love has nothing to do
With ugly or beautiful, big or small
It's a matter of your heart
And if it has a wall

True love has nothing to do
With age, height, and weight
It's a matter of your heart
And if it has a blind spot

2/19/2013

JESUS HAS RISEN

Hallelujah, Jesus Is Alive!
What an amazing love He has for us
To die for sinners who deny and hate you
We can never imagine the depth your love

Jesus, you have God's nature
And are God Himself
You humbled yourself
To take a human form

Became an offering sacrifice
To die on the cross for us
Through your precious blood
The curtain of the temple was torn in two

Through your precious blood
We are clean and without blemish
The veil and barrier are destroyed
So now we can reconcile with God

You have brought us into God's kingdom
In one spirit of Jesus Christ
And now we are no longer servants of sin
But adopted sons of yours

You rose again to bring
Us eternal hope
The law is only a shadow
Of the coming good things

You have become a reality
For us to follow your steps
Our current world is also
A shadow of the coming good things

We will die and rise with you
In a whole new world
In Heaven you will wipe out our tears
And we will enjoy the eternal happiness

3/30/2013

COLOR OUR BOOK OF LIFE

May our life in the Book
Of Life of God
Bloom like the flower
The best part of the good

Full of the happiness
And of the joy
Until we finish our journey
And move on to the next eternity

4/7/2013

A Moment Of Thoughts

Trust is built by daily activities
Instead of a one time promise
Trust is a relationship
Not merchandise with a warranty

Some things we know are wrong
But still want to pursue
Because we are persistent
And we don't want to give up our pride

Some people are meant
To pass through our life
But not to stay in our life
And we should let them go

6/1/2013

WAIT ON THE LORD FOR HIS JUSTICE

How can you be happy
During the trial
It's seems as if
It is almost impossible!

As long as you keep calm
It's already good enough
And you should be
Proud of yourself

How can you have peace
When there is no justice?
It's seems as if
It is definitely impossible!

You are not a cold person
Instead you have a loving heart
Given in grace to you
From God's Holy Spirit

His Spirit stirs
Your heart to see
Write and act as if until
His justice carries it out

6/21/2013

LEAVE ALL THINGS BEHIND

I left all things behind
Which once dragged me down
I wiped my own tears away
Grabbing anything to stand

Crawling just to move ahead
I cannot and must not stay
Must keep moving on
With no hesitation

Life is too short
And I am getting old
Time runs out fast
And never comes back

I almost forgot God's calling
I'm trying to hold on
I was born with nothing
And I will go home without anything

I must move on now
And leave all things behind
That once dragged me down
And leave all things behind

7/3/2013

COMMUNICATION IS ESSENTIAL

When we have different
Opinions with each other
It doesn't cause conflict
If we communicate with respect

But when we hold to our pride
And our hallucinated assumptions
Our communication develops wrong motives
And we create enemies amongst ourselves

7/10/2013

LOVE HAS NO ENDING

Love has no age
Keep spreading our love
And our peace and truth
Forever and ever

That's all we must do
Because that's our purpose in life

9/8/2013

WE ARE ONE BODY IN JESUS CHRIST

Friendship is the treasure
I have in you

How beautiful it is
We are in one body

It is a mysterious story
But it is all true

Thanks to Jesus, In Him
All believers sing the same tune

10/4/2013

MY THANKSGIVING PRAYER

Thank You Lord
For everyday sunlight
And direction in the darkness
With the bright moonlight

Thank you Lord
For family and friends
When we are in the valley
To provide us our strength

Thank you Lord
For Your living water and food
You have quenched our thirst
And satisfied all we need

Thank you Lord

11/27/2013

LIFE IS LIKE FOUR SEASONS

Life is like
Four different seasons
You cannot explain
The cause for any reasons

If we have tried our best
But still cannot change
Just accept and enjoy
Nature's beauty and dance

12/1/2013

JESUS WAS BORN JUST FOR US

You are the best gift given
In all of human history
You came down from heaven
Disregarding your glory out of love

You bring us eternal peace
Love, joy, hope and life
In You, we have been rescued
From darkness, death, struggles and grief

There are so many signs
Showing that you are the Messiah
The years start counting
Right after your birth

We had never seen God
Or touched God's love
Now we can feel
Your gentle touch as a dove

Oh, Lord! We are not
Celebrating only your birth
We also meditate how important
It is to all human life

So that we can follow
In your perfect footsteps
And work to carry out
Your Holy element in depth

Peace on earth
Are not the words
Accepting Jesus
Is the true way to peace

12/24/2013

ACKNOWLEDGMENTS

If we believe in miracles, then miracles do happen every day. It's only a matter of recognizing them or not. I believe that Anthony Duhamel Jr. is a gift and a miracle from God. I met Anthony at Starbucks. When I was sending a message to a Facebook friend, I asked him to proofread my message. He was kind enough to do so, and I immediately felt that he was a Christian. I started to chat with him, and it turned out that my instinct was right. I also noticed that he was using the same graphic program that I was using, so we were able to share and exchange our interests. Before I left, we exchanged our personal information and added each other on Facebook.

After I returned home, I had strong feelings that urged me to contact him. I have written many poems over the years to relieve my feelings of sadness during hardships. Also, since I was young, I have always wanted to be a writer and publish my books.

I had never had strong feelings to ask someone's help to publish my poetry, but I decided to follow the prompting of the Holy Spirit and asked him for his help. To my surprise, Anthony returned my message with a very positive response. Although he is not an expert and still learning the publishing process, he was also inspired and touched by the Spirit and has been willing to help me at no charge and without any hesitations.

Anthony also introduced me to his wife, Rachel Duhamel. Since our first meeting in January up until now, both Anthony and Rachel are helping me to proofread my poems, design book covers and layouts, and publish in both print and eBook versions. Although Anthony is learning the process and working on the book at the same time, he is a fast learner, professional, and creative. He is a good young man with lots of love in his heart for God and his friends. I thank God for sending Anthony and Rachel to me, and I cannot thank them more. Words are just not enough for me to express my appreciation for them. May God bless you Anthony and Rachel!

- Mei Esther Wang

About The Author

Mei Esther Wang was born and raised in Taiwan. At age 15, her parents passed away, leaving her to take care of herself. Through her strength, determination, and close relationship with God, she turned an almost impossible situation into a story of inspiration and victory. Leaving her job on an assembly line at age 23, she was determined to finish her education. Through the aid of a Christian missionary organization, she was able to complete her high school and undergraduate college education. She then made the bold decision to emigrate to the United States in 1993 and proceeded to earn Masters Degrees from Azuza Pacific University and CSU Los Angeles. She currently resides in Alhambra, CA.

Transforming in God's Plan is her first published work.

You can contact Mei and follow her journey at these social media outlets:

www.facebook.com/mei.wang1

www.twitter.com/meiestherwang

www.ingramcontent.com/pod-product-compliance
Lightning Source LLC
Chambersburg PA
CBHW061158040426
42445CB00013B/1717